A Hiker's Guide to the Rachel Carson Trail

A 35.7 mile day hiking trail in Allegheny County, Pennsylvania

© 2005 Rachel Carson Trails Conservancy, Inc.
All rights reserved

Fourth Edition
By Steve Mentzer
November, 2004

Rachel Carson Trails Conservancy, Inc.
P.O. Box 35
Warrendale, PA 15086-0035
info@rachelcarsontrails.org

Rachel Carson photographs courtesy of the Lear/Carson Collection, Connecticut College

Front Cover: The Rachel Carson Trail follows a woodchip path along Deer Creek in Emmerling Park, Indiana Township. Photograph by Don Erdeljac.

Table of Contents

The Rachel Carson Trail 1
Trail Use and Ethics 2
Navigating the Trail 3
Recollections 4
Rachel Carson 5
The Rachel Carson Trails Conservancy 7
Trail Description West to East 9
Trail Description East to West 17
Section 1: Western Terminus to Route 8 25
Section 2: Route 8 to Shaffer Road 26
Section 3: Shaffer Road to Cove Run Road 27
Section 4: Cove Run Road to Yutes Run Road 28
Section 5: Yutes Run Road to Bailey Run Road 29
Section 6: Bailey Run Road to Burtner Road 30
Section 7: Burtner Road to Eastern Terminus 31
Table of GPS Coordinates 32
Directions to the Trailheads 33
Index 34

The Rachel Carson Trail

The Rachel Carson Trail is a 35.7 mile (57.4 km) hiking trail lying entirely within Allegheny County, north of Pittsburgh. The trail was conceived and built by the Pittsburgh Council, American Youth Hostels.

In 1950 the Pittsburgh Council dedicated the Baker Trail, a foot trail extending from the Highland Park Bridge, Pittsburgh, to Cook Forest State Park, more than 100 miles north. Sometime thereafter, the 25 miles within Allegheny County were abandoned largely due to development of the Allegheny Valley Expressway (Route 28). Today the Baker Trail extends from Freeport to the Allegheny National Forest, 141 miles long and shares part of its treadway with the North Country Trail.

From 1972 to 1975 members of the AYH scouted and rebuilt much of the former trail which follows the bluffs of the Allegheny River. The trail picks up the old trail in Harrison Hills County Park and continues to Springdale and then Harwick.

Around Harwick, the old trail was disrupted by road construction. But, it generally follows a gas pipeline to Dorseyville, where it crosses the Pennsylvania Turnpike. The Rachel Carson Trail skirts Hartwood Acres County Park with a short spur entering the park, the former Lawrence estate. The trail proceeds west to North Park, including almost a mile in the Hampton Nature Reserve. Roads are avoided as much as possible, traversing three County parks and several township parks, most established since 1950.

Because the trail passes close by the birthplace of Rachel Carson, in Springdale, and because of the interest of the AYH membership in the environment, the Pittsburgh Council decided to name the trail after one of the early ecologists. Rachel Carson was the author of *The Sea Around Us* and *Silent Spring*. (See the brief biography and bibliography elsewhere in this Guide.)

The Rachel Carson Trail has been blazed with yellow paint in the form of standard 2 inch by 6 inch rectangles. Wooden signs with yellow lettering identify the trail at several road crossings and in the County parks.

An extension of the original trail has been blazed north through North Park from the former Rocky Dell Shelter to a point behind the Beaver Shelter.

THE CHALLENGE

Each year on the Saturday nearest the summer solstice, hundreds of hikers take part in the Rachel Carson Trail Challenge wherein they attempt to hike virtually the entire trail in one day. Checkpoints every 6-7 miles provide water and snacks, and a cookout at the finish serves up hamburgers and hot dogs to the weary. For details on this event, visit the trail web site at http://www.rachelcarsontrails.org.

Trail Use and Ethics

The Rachel Carson Trail is intended to be used exclusively by hikers; permission of landowners was obtained on this basis. Boy Scouts, Girl Scouts, families, other groups and individuals are welcome to walk the trail.

The trail exists and is maintained for day-hiking purposes; there are no shelters or camps along the way. The privilege of camping on private land may be requested of the landowner; Allegheny County bans camping in its parks. Water should be carried by hikers.

This trail is relatively primitive and is steep in places; no bridges have been built so streams have to be crossed as is.

TRAIL ETHICS

Please:

- **Be courteous to people living along the trail.**
- **Remember, you are hiking generally on private property.**
- **Respect the land and its owners. If asked to leave, do so.**
- **Stay on the trail.**
- **Do not camp or build fires along the trail.**
- **Refrain from bringing dogs and bicycles on the trail.**
- **Keep off the trail with motorized vehicles.**
- **Carry out your own trash; help by picking up others' litter.**
- **Recognize your limitations and your assumed risk. The Rachel Carson Trails Conservancy and the landowners want you to enjoy your hike; neither will take the responsibility for personal injury or losses while using the trail.**

TRAIL SAFETY

Several steep and potentially dangerous cliffs border the trail. The bluffs are scenic but also risky. Children should be watched carefully. As well, about 9.5 miles of the trail is along roads. Most of these are lightly travelled, but some carry fast-moving traffic and have dangerous curves. Please use extreme caution at all times. Yield for traffic and never assume drivers can see you.

Know where you are at all times, along with nearby access roads. Bring a cell phone with you while hiking and dial 911 in an emergency. However, cell service may be poor in some valleys. Although it can feel like it, you are never very far from civilization. Considering carrying a whistle to alert rescuers to your location.

Navigating the Trail

Rectangular yellow blazes 2" by 6" painted on trees, telephone poles, guardrails, and so forth mark the route of the Rachel Carson Trail. Understanding the different types of blazes is essential in order to properly follow the trail and prevent getting lost.

There are two different blazing types used on the trail. A "single" blaze indicates that you are following the trail. A "double" blaze indicates a change in the trail (think of it as a kind of alert). This convention is used on most hiking trails.

TRAIL MARKERS

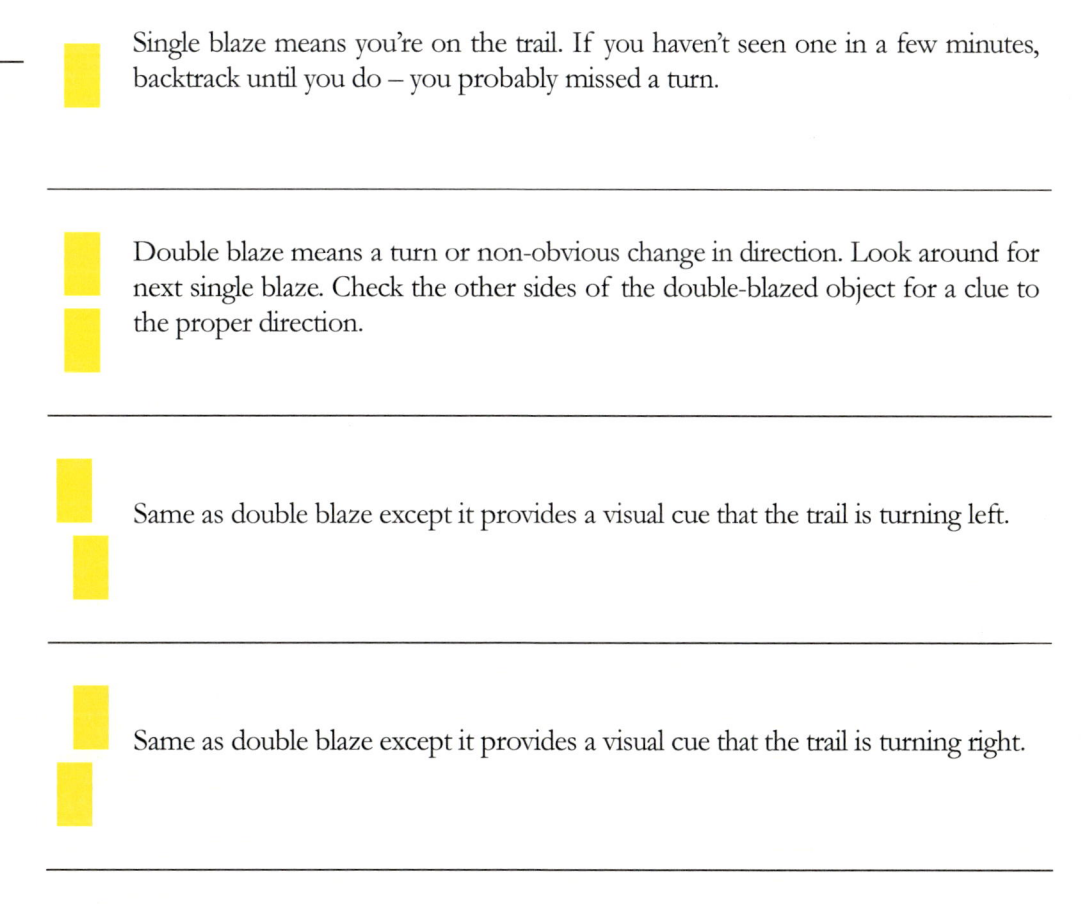

Single blaze means you're on the trail. If you haven't seen one in a few minutes, backtrack until you do – you probably missed a turn.

Double blaze means a turn or non-obvious change in direction. Look around for next single blaze. Check the other sides of the double-blazed object for a clue to the proper direction.

Same as double blaze except it provides a visual cue that the trail is turning left.

Same as double blaze except it provides a visual cue that the trail is turning right.

Recollections

On the first anniversary of the Rachel Carson Trail

By Joe Levine, from the 1976 edition

One year ago in February, 1975, Cliff and Marilyn Ham and I blazed the final segments that completed the Rachel Carson Trail. For a hiking trail practically on the city's doorstep, it is extremely varied, even quite primitive in places. The trail traverses several county parks, follows power and gas lines, skirts suburban homes and farms, crosses creeks, meanders through woods and fields and passes steep bluffs. All 33 miles are within Allegheny County.

About four years ago, the project got under way. Cliff Ham spent endless hours getting permission from property owners along the proposed route. Many AYHer's as well as other individuals and groups were involved. There were several exploratory hikes in '72 and '73 led by Cliff and Marilyn and George and Gladys Schubert. I participated in one such memorable week-end of trail finding and blazing in the fall of '74.

The group worked north from Tarentum and camped in Harrison Hills Park with a troop of Boy Scouts. The following day we routed the trail south from Tarentum to Glassmere. Ah, who can forget the bramble patches? Or those cardiac hills that follow the power line north of Tarentum? Remember, the fellow who zipped a black snake into the pocket of his knapsack ... the disagreeable trail-biker near Creighton ... the Saturday night thunderstorm ... and indefatigable Cliff Ham scouting around and ahead, while the rest of us barely kept up with him, following his blazes?

Bruce Schenker, wife Evelyn, and son scouted the route from North Park's Rocky Dell Shelter to County Park Nine[1]. Hard labor converted a hillside along Crouse Run into a trail. Friendly Bruce wangled permission from all the landowners.

Well, the trail was completed and has been open to all hikers, but there is work to be done. Occasionally, sections have been disrupted by road construction or by new unsympathetic property owners. Sections have to be re-routed. A connecting leg between County Park Nine[1] and the Highland Park Bridge has to be explored. Areas need to be blazed and new extensions are being planned.

It's fun to reminisce on past events and past trips, but it is equally enjoyable to anticipate the fun of future trips. The Rachel Carson Trail still needs our attention and effort to keep it viable. Happy Anniversary Rachel Carson Trail.

[1] **Now Hartwood Acres County Park.**

Rachel Carson

Rachel Louise Carson, marine biologist, author of *Silent Spring*, and early ecologist, was born at 613 Marion Avenue, Springdale, Allegheny County, Pennsylvania in 1907. Twenty-two years later, after finishing high school and the Pennsylvania College for Women (now Chatham College), she earned a Master's degree in Zoology from Johns Hopkins University. She taught several years at Johns Hopkins Summer School and at the University of Maryland. In 1936 she became a "junior aquatic biologist" with the Bureau of Fisheries (later part of the Fish and Wildlife Service of the Department of the Interior). An early essay, written as an outgrowth of her relationship with the Bureau, was "Undersea", published by Atlantic Monthly, September, 1937.

Rachel Carson in 1962

Rachel Carson's first major work was *Under the Sea Wind* (Simon & Shuster, 1951). She continued to work in the Fish & Wildlife Service, one of the few professionally-trained women employed there. Her responsibility was publications, her title "Biologist". She admirably united the knowledge of a scientist with the skills of a writer. During this period she edited twelve "Conservation in Action" booklets, including "Plum Island", "Chincoteague" and "Mattamuskeet". In July of 1951, *The Sea Around Us*, for which Ms. Carson received the National Book Award, was published by Oxford Press. This book was on the best seller list for many months; a new edition of *Under the Sea Wind* was published at this time and joined the first on the best seller list.

During all her years of studying, writing, and serving the Fish and Wildlife Service, Ms. Carson was an active hiker, bird watcher, outdoors explorer, and nature enthusiast. In 1945 she visited Hawk Mountain, Pennsylvania; other trips included Plum Island, the Everglades, the Maine Coast, and late in her life, the California redwoods.

Rachel Carson at Hawk Mountain in 1946

In January 1958 a letter published in a Boston paper stimulated Rachel Carson to warn of the dangers of herbicides and pesticides, DDT, and other chemicals. Her book, published in 1962 as *Silent Spring*, required several years of detailed research, tedious hours of writing, and considerable controversy. During the process, Ms. Carson was informed that she had metastasized cancer, in addition to ulcers and other health troubles. Publication of *Silent Spring* brought overwhelmingly favorable response although industry, *Time* magazine, and *Readers Digest* attacked the book, its findings, and its author. President Kennedy appointed a "Pesticides Committee" whose report in May 1963 supported *Silent Spring* and criticized industry and the laxness of several agencies in the Federal government. Ms. Carson's book has been published in many languages and editions, and has brought general awareness of the dangers of even limited use of chemical fertilizers, herbicides, fungicides, and other products which affect nature.

Rachel Carson died in April 1964 at the age of 56. In 1980 she was awarded the Presidential Medal of Freedom by President Carter. The house at 613 Marion Avenue in Springdale, PA has been restored as the Rachel Carson Homestead by the Rachel Carson Homestead Association. The Association's telephone number is (412) 274-5459, or you may send email to rcarson@salsgiver.com; or visit their web site at http://www.rachelcarsonhomestead.org.

> "For all at last return to the sea---
> to Oceanus, the ocean river,
> like the everflowing stream of time,
> the beginning and the end."
> -from *The Sea Around Us*

The Rachel Carson Trails Conservancy

Preserving and Promoting Community Trails in Western Pennsylvania

The Rachel Carson Trails Conservancy, Inc. is a volunteer-run organization dedicated to the development, protection, and promotion of hiking, biking, and walking trails throughout western Pennsylvania.

OUR HISTORY

Founded in 1992 as the Harmony Trails Council, its mission was to develop, promote, establish and maintain a multi-use public trail system as an alternate transportation and recreation facility serving the residents of Pittsburgh's North Hills, focusing on the railbed of the former Harmony inter-urban rail line. In 2004, the Pittsburgh chapter of Hostelling International (formerly AYH) elected to relinquish its stewardship of the Rachel Carson Trail and the Baker Trail. The Harmony Trails Council chose to adopt these trails thereby expanding its mission. At the same time, the Council voted to change its name to the Rachel Carson Trails Conservancy to better reflect its broader mission.

GET INVOLVED

The organization meets monthly in Warrendale, PA and has many opportunities for volunteers willing to contribute their time. From meeting with local officials about trail development and protection to participating in a trail work crew, creating newsletter or web content, communicating with the press, or volunteering for the Rachel Carson Trail Challenge, the possibilities are as varied as the backgrounds of the people involved. For more information, contact Marian Crossman at (412) 366-3339 or email info@rachelcarsontrails.org or visit the web site at www.rachelcarsontrails.org.

Trail Description West to East

SECTION 1: WESTERN TERMINUS TO ROUTE 8
4.3 mi. (6.9 km)

The western terminus of the Rachel Carson Trail is located off Babcock Boulevard in North Park behind the Beaver Shelter. To reach it, follow the Yellow Belt to North Park and turn north on Babcock Boulevard at its intersection with Ingomar Road and Wildwood Road. There is a parking lot on the left at the next intersection with Pearce Mill Road and the Beaver Shelter is at the far (north) end of the lot [Parking WT]. This shelter is also a terminus of the annual Rachel Carson Trail Challenge (described on page 1). Walk by the shelter, away from Babcock Boulevard, cross the causeway and turn left down toward the lake and over a stream feeding the lake. In the woods, look right and you'll see the "Rachel Carson Trail" [Western Terminus] signpost, the western terminus of the Trail. You may alternatively continue past the sign and follow the well-defined bridle trail all the way to the North Park Skating Rink, another 2.2 miles further. It has been reported (9/97) that maps of North Park incorrectly show the bridle trail leading to the Skating Rink as the Rachel Carson Trail. Otherwise, turn left and follow the Trail, blazed with traffic yellow 2" by 6" rectangles toward Pearce Mill Road. This area in here is usually low and soggy.

Note
Throughout this guide text in brackets, e.g. [Parking WT], indicates a reference to this location on the corresponding map for this trail section.

At Pearce Mill Road (also Pierce Mill Road), turn left, walk toward Babcock Boulevard [Babcock Boulevard], cross it and turn right toward North Park Lake spillway. Immediately before the spillway bridge, turn left and drop down along the spillway, which feeds Pine Creek. Cross Pine Creek over a bridge and enter The Mansions condominium development along a dirt service road and turn right when you reach the paved driveway for the development. This will lead out to a junction with Wildwood Road [Wildwood Road]. Cross Wildwood Road and continue on a park road for a short distance, then turn left and head up the hillside into North Park, passing the Connolly Shelter on your far right. The Trail continues through the woods and in quick succession passes to the left and behind the Massachusetts Shelter and then to the right of the Tupelo Shelter. You then pass to the rear and to the left of the Harmar Shelter. Soon you see the Honeysuckle Shelter on your left with the road to your right, then the Triple Oak Shelter to your left. The Trail will cross a paved road at a point 50 yards to the left of the Woods Athletic Field and cut a course across that road that is about halfway between the Lilac Shelter on your right and the Jeanette Shelter on your left. Head to the left of the Elwood Shelter and in about 100 yards pass to the right of the Beveridge Shelter. Cross the paved road, through a short stretch of woods and down the dirt service road to the paved Hemlocks Drive III.

Turn left, go 50 yards or so along the road and turn right down to the abandoned Rocky Dell Shelter [Rocky Dell Shelter] in North Park. The rocky ledges in the shelter area are worth a few photographs. Follow the stream all the way to the railroad tracks. Turn right along the tracks and follow the Trail keeping to the right (south) side of the tracks. In about a quarter mile, turn left on Sample Road (this area is called Sample Station) and cross Pine Creek on a bridge; continue 250 yards along Sample Road

[Sample Road] to a small gravel parking area [Sample Road Parking] where the Trail turns left into the woods then descends into the Crouse Run area (you will observe the grade of the former Pittsburgh-to-Butler Interurban running parallel to Crouse Run). The Trail crosses Crouse Run several times (wet crossings), going onto and off the railroad grade. The Trail emerges into a private backyard where it turns left and around a gate ("No Trespassing" signs may be posted) then crosses a small gravel roadway [Indian Springs Lane]. It then passes closely behind several houses and a detention pond to your right in the dense bushes, and soon intersects PA Route 8 [Route 8].

SECTION 2: ROUTE 8 TO SHAFFER ROAD
3.2 mi (5.1 km)

Cross Route 8. The safest way to do this is to go to the stop light at the intersection to your left, about 200 yards down the road. This is a heavily traveled road with fast-moving traffic. The Trail follows a private driveway directly opposite the pathway to Route 8, just south of a car dealership. This area is known as Talley Cavey. Once you are across Route 8 follow the power line uphill and onto Hampton Middle School property. Turn right and follow along the right side of the roadway parallel to the school building on your left. Along here you see a nice place for a break or lunch, under the shade trees on the school lawn. At the intersection of Topnick Drive and School Road [School Road] the Trail turns right down a pipeline clearing for about 30 yards, then turns left into the woods. The Trail comes out to a paved road [Topnick Drive] where you go over the guardrail, turn right along the road then left into more woods in less than 100 yards. The Trail emerges onto a grassy service road, turns right and passes a small section of guardrail into an open field, which is Hampton Township school property. Follow along the left edge of the field for about 100 feet then turn left into the woods, which is the Hampton Nature Reserve. Follow the Trail in this Reserve for more than a mile, first to a utility right-of-way then downhill over a footbridge, cross a small stream at the bottom of the hill, and then uphill to McCully Road [McCully Road]. Turn left on McCully Road and cross Middle Road [Middle Road] onto Cedar Run Road. About 50 yards down, just before the road bears left, the Trail turns right at a telephone pole. Follow the tree line on the left while heading up the hill onto a wide path and up to a 1300 ft. knob on a cleared hilltop. Bear left and follow the Trail into the woods and down to another wide path adjacent to an open field.

Hartwood Acres spur

At this point, where the Trail emerges from the woods, Hartwood Acres can be reached by a trail going off from this point to the other side (south) of Wagner Road. Look for a 4"x4" post with a red band around it. Head down the hill and across the field to the next red blaze on a pole. At Wagner road turn left and then right down Edgehill Drive. At the back end of Edgehill Drive (see a sign "TRAIL" with an arrow), follow up a dirt path to the right which leads off behind the paved driveway, then on the limestone chip road to the left of the corral fence and up to the Hartwood Acres mansion. The spur exits into an open grassy area behind a dome shaped maintenance building, several hundred feet from the mansion.

Proceed along the tree line to your left to a small private lake [Hidden Pond]. This is an excellent spot to enjoy lunch in the small pavilion built by the owner, Nicola DiCio. Follow along the right edge of the lake, down a small rise and into an open field. Stay along the right edge and head straight across toward the woods ahead. Please stay on the Trail in this area and do not approach the houses (the landowners here appreciate their privacy). Enter the woods and make your way down along the creek, keeping it to your left. Cross over a dirt bridge (atop a large pipe) into a grassy field and continue to parallel the creek which will now be on your right. The Trail will stay to the left of a small pond then turn left on the unpaved Wagner Road [Wagner Road], at the right edge of a parking area. (Do not park your car here, it's private property.) Turn right on Church Lane [Church Lane] then left on Shaffer Road [Shaffer Road].

SECTION 3: SHAFFER ROAD TO COVE RUN ROAD
4.6 mi. (7.4 km)

Follow Shaffer Road, a lightly traveled gravel road that ends when it intersects the paved Cedar Run Road [Cedar Run Road]. Continue straight on Cedar Run Road until it intersects Route 910 [Route 910]. Cross 910, turn right and follow the road until just past the first private residence on the left, just before a section of guardrail begins. The Trail turns left into the woods and crosses property owned by Tom Eichenlaub. It emerges on Saxonburg Boulevard near Dorseyville [Saxonburg Boulevard], turns left and continues along this road for 0.5 miles, crossing over the Pennsylvania Turnpike and Deer Creek.

About 50 feet beyond the Deer Creek bridge, the Trail turns right over the guardrail and down into the open, grassy field in front of a crane equipment company [Casey Equipment]. Walk diagonally across the field toward the gate at the paved driveway entrance. Pass through the gate and walk along the driveway, continuing straight off the driveway and into the equipment tool yard (stay off the equipment). The Trail enters the woods at the back of the yard and, after about 50 yards, crosses a small stream called Cunningham Run (usually a wet crossing) and continues past a pipeline swath that ascends steeply up the hill to your right. In May, look for spectacular European columbine along here and the road that follows.

In a short distance the Trail turns right up the hill along a rugged path and emerges onto Eisele Road [Eisele Road]. Turn right and follow Eisele Road down, past Camp Deer Creek and the soccer fields, to its intersection with Cove Run Road. Cross the road and enter into Emmerling Park, an Indiana Township Park with rest rooms, picnic shelters, and ball fields. After crossing the footbridge over Deer Creek into the parking lot, turn left back toward the creek and follow the woodchip path along it. Cross Deer Creek again using the bridge [Deer Creek Bridge] installed by Indiana Township and head up the hill through a magnificent stand of hemlocks. This section of the Trail is shared with trail bikes and some of the bike ruts in this area are quite deep. After a while the Trail makes a sharp right turn, continues up the hill and soon crosses Cove Run Road [Cove Run Road] again.

SECTION 4: COVE RUN ROAD TO YUTES RUN ROAD
3.1 mi. (5 km)

Cross Cove Run Road, up the hill through the woods to the top then down the other side. Before reaching the bottom, the Trail turns left, crosses two small streams then heads back up the hill. It descends again to Long Run, a beautiful section which is full of wildflowers in spring (notably fire pinks and trillium). Unfortunately this area has been attacked by trail bikes, but you can enjoy the wildflowers alongside the Trail anyway. Follow to the left of Long Run to the pipeline swath at the base of Rich Hill. Turn right, cross Long Run [Long Run] and make your way up this treacherous ascent to Rich Hill Road [Rich Hill Road]. Cross Rich Hill Road and continue straight ahead along the pipeline. A dirt service road will cross perpendicular to the pipeline, at which point the Trail turns right and follows the road. The road will end at a chain link fence and the Trail continues, keeping to the left edge of the fence and emerging on a paved road which leads to a fly ash dump site. Walk down the road about 150 yards and turn right off the road, up and into the woods. The Trail will exit the woods onto another pipeline swath at the top of LaFever Hill and turn left. Follow the pipeline down past an A-frame house and a driveway leading out to LaFever Hill Road [LaFever Hill Road]. Turn left and go under a railroad bridge to Little Deer Creek Road, also called Russellton Road. Cross Little Deer Creek Road onto Log Cabin Road [Log Cabin Road] for about 30 yards or so, then turn right again onto the pipeline swath steeply ascending the hill. Follow the gas pipeline up the steep hill and eventually you will descend to Yutes Run Road [Yutes Run Road].

SECTION 5: YUTES RUN ROAD TO BAILEY RUN ROAD
8.9 mi. (14.3 km)

Turn right on Yutes Run Road [Yutes Run Road] and follow it 0.7 miles to its intersection with Tawney Run Road [Tawney Run Road], going under the Route 28 overpass in Harwick. Turn left on Tawney Run Road and, after about 100 yards or so, bear left up an incline onto an old railroad bed which parallels Tawney Run Road. After about 400 yards, turn sharply right, drop down, cross Tawney Run Road and enter the woods on the other side. After a short distance you will cross Tawney Run and head up the hill. When the Trail reaches a dirt road, turn left, then after about 50 yards, turn right, up a pipeline swath toward the orange globe marking the pipeline at the top of the hill. At the globe you will be next to the house owned by Jim Drummond,. Continue out to the paved driveway and turn right, passing the greenhouse area of the former Peterson's Nursery, down to Butler Road [Butler Road]. Cross Butler Road and follow the Trail through an attractive wooded area owned by William Shaul, who at one time was the milkman for the Carson family.

The Trail will emerge on yet another pipeline/powerline swath, turn left and follow it. The Trail goes up and down like a roller coaster several times along here. After about 1.1 miles, you'll see the chain link fence surrounding playing fields for Springdale High School on your right [Springdale HS Fields].

Rachel Carson Homestead spur

To reach the Rachel Carson Homestead [Rachel Carson Homestead], walk along the perimeter of the chain link fence, heading away from the power line tower with a red band around it and following the red blazes on the posts. At the paved road, Butler Street, turn right and in about 200 yards left on Marion Avenue. Continue for 1.5 blocks and you will see

> the Homestead on the right side of the street, at 613 Marion Avenue. If you had turned left on Butler Street and walked downhill, you would have reached, in less than a block, the spring after which Springdale is named, still providing cold, clear spring water for thirsty hikers. The Homestead has been converted to an "ecology education center and museum". Springdale's pollution-monitoring station is located in the backyard.

Continue walking downhill along the pipeline/power line until you reach Freeport Road [Freeport Road] in Springdale. Turn left and at the next intersection with Riddle Run Road [Riddle Run Road] (called Springdale Hollow Road on some maps), cross this road and bear left up the powerline swath. After turning right off the power line and into the woods and then back to the power line again, you will be in Agan Park. Although it is not evident that you are in a park, the park area offers a peaceful setting where you can take a break and (in the spring) enjoy the wildflowers. This section of the Trail along the bluffs offers terrific views of Arnold, New Kensington and Parnassus. In the distance one can see Lower Burrell and Plum Boro. Continue along the bluffs, observing the New Kensington bridge crossing the Allegheny River below. The Trail soon turns left away from the bluffs, swings left and goes down a dirt service road. After about 1/3 mile it intersects with another dirt road leading up to the park ball fields. Turn right on this road and follow it down, through the entrance gate, to the Agan Park [Agan Park Entrance] on Riddle Run Road.

Turn right (north) on Riddle Run Road and follow it 0.8 miles to Murray Hill Road and turn right again. After 0.2 miles, bear right off the road and down a jeep trail. About 25 yards down, the Trail makes a sharp left into the woods and in only 150 yards or so comes out into a field occupied by a tall radio tower [Murray Hill Tower]. Turn left and approach Murray Hill Estates, crossing two roads in the development and threading between backyards. Proceed down the power line cut, turning left into the woods then back out to the power line. Follow the transmission lines downhill and then uphill. As you near the end of the cut the Trail makes a dramatic drop down to Murray Hill Road [Murray Hill Road]. (There may be a cable along the left tree line to assist you along here.) Turn right on Murray Hill Road for about 200 yards and turn left into a gravel parking lot behind a former school. Go through the schoolyard, crossing Crawford Run on a small footbridge.

This is a good spot to take a break if you are so inclined. There is a convenience store [Sheetz] adjacent to the schoolyard with food, drinks, and restrooms.

When you are ready to continue, turn left onto Crawford Run Road [Crawford Run Road] in Creighton, past the highway ramp coming out on your left and follow the blazes along the road, staying on the sidewalk on the left side, under the overpass, about 225 yards total, to just across from a small gravel parking area on the opposite side of the road. The Trail crosses the road here and heads up an old service road. When the ground begins to level out the Trail turns left into the woods, up an incline and more woods, and emerges on yet another steep power line swath. Not far after reaching the top, the Trail turns left into the woods through an area that is covered with deep blue dayflowers with yellow whiskers in the summer. As you come out into a power line clearing, enjoy the panoramic view to your left (north).

The Trail crosses the clearing somewhat diagonally and re-enters the woods. After about 0.4 miles, as you approach a farm area (the farm of Jack Bailey), follow the blazes as the Trail takes a long detour around the farm clearing, keeping the farm to your left, going through a wooded area. The Trail continues down and around the steep hillside and, as you approach the bottom along the bed of a small stream descending through a crease in the hillside, passes a number of junk automobiles. Continue down and cross Bailey Run without using a bridge (usually a wet crossing), climb up and over the guardrail to Bailey Run Road [Bailey Run Road]. **Do not use any of the bridges of the local residents!**

SECTION 6: BAILEY RUN ROAD TO BURTNER ROAD
4.9 mi. (7.9 km)

Turn right (south) on Bailey Run Road and continue right at its intersection with Days Run Road. After about 250 yards, the Trail turns left off the road, past an abandoned house and the property of Roy Collins, ascends a long hill up to a power line and turns left. The Trail leaves the power line, keeps to the right of a PPG tailings area., past another great view of the valley and a telecommunications tower. Soon the Trail will parallel a fence at a point just above St. Clemens Cemetery [St. Clemens Cemetery] then zig-zags a couple of times as it descend the hillside to Bakerstown Road. This hillside is often thickly overgrown with brambles.

Turn right on Bakerstown Road for 30 yards or so then, just turn left over the guardrail and head down the wooded hillside. This area is delightful in the summer and fall. The Trail crosses a creek at the bottom, then goes to the right and switchbacks up the hillside. It emerges on a jeep road, turns right and follows it out to the top of the ridge [Tarentum Overlook], which is a good spot to stop and enjoy the view of Route 28, exit number 14, and the town of Tarentum. When you are ready to leave follow the path down, parallel to and within full view of the Expressway, to an open area. Cross the open area heading toward the Expressway and a cluster of trees adjacent to it. The Trail continues down and back up the hillside covered with crown vetch. The vetch is often quite thick, so take care not to get entangled. At the bottom of this stretch Bull Creek passes underneath you and the Expressway. At Bull Creek Road [Bull Creek Road] cross over the guardrail, turn left for approximately 220 yards, then turn right on Ridge Road [Ridge Road].

Continue on Ridge Road for 1.3 miles to just beyond a farm on your right. Turn right down a gravel driveway and past a gate. Before the driveway bears left the Trail angles right off it, up a small incline and into the woods. This section of the Trail is ablaze with fall colors in October. The Trail will turn left ahead, then reach a power line and follow it to the right. Soon the Trail will descend the power line steeply and, after crossing a creek at the bottom, reach Burtner Road [Burtner Road].

SECTION 7: BURTNER ROAD TO EASTERN TERMINUS
6.8 mi. (10.9 km)

Cross Burtner Road and ascend the steep hill on the other side. Along the top the Trail follows a gravel service road that parallels the power line and follows it left as it turns off it. Soon the Trail emerges on another power line clearing which it follows for a short distance before turning right into the woods. Spot the blazes! The Trail comes back to the power line clearing and crosses over to the other side. It loops through the woods and comes back to the power line clearing again; cross directly in a straight line to the other side and find the blazes. Again the Trail loops through the woods and comes back on the power line clearing for the last time. Walk directly straight ahead across to the other side of the power line clearing. Continue a short distance and turn right along a dirt service road. Shortly you encounter a cell tower. Continue along right of the tower onto the cell tower service road leading downhill. In the fall the oaks and maples lining both sides of this lane are especially beautiful.

At Donnelville Road [Donnelville Road], turn right (north) to Saxonburg Road [Saxonburg Road], the first road you encounter and again turn right (east). Walk along the right side of Saxonburg Road; go under the double overpass of Route 28. Turn left onto Alter Road [Alter Road] and follow it 0.2 miles to a gravel driveway on the right shared by several houses. Turn right and follow the driveway past the houses, continuing straight when it turns to dirt at the last house on the left. Climb to the top of the hill (elevation: 1300 ft.) and pass through the barbed wire, going in and then leaving a corral [Corral] for the horses.

The Trail continues through the woods and follows a dirt service road for a time as it proceeds downhill to a marshy area at the bottom of the hill. Cross the small creek and proceed up the steep hill onto a gas line swath that doubles as an old dirt road. Turn left and follow this up to Altermoor Road [Altermoor Road] and turn right. Proceed for 1.5 blocks and turn right along a small side road running parallel to Freeport Road, directly across Freeport Road from the Harrison Hills Volunteer Fire Department, and follow it to Freeport Road.

Cross Freeport Road into Harrison Hills County Park, about 50 yards the north of the Park entrance [HH Park Entrance]. The Trail crosses the left fork of the main park road and follows the right one for about 250 yards before turning right into a clearing. It goes through a picnic shelters and skirts a small pond in which beavers have lived [Beaver Pond] before climbing a modest hill and turning right. In a short distance it will cross the service road leading to the soccer fields and will eventually emerge at the Bobwhite shelter, a terminus of the annual Rachel Carson Trail Challenge (described on page 1) and another place to locate the Trail [Bobwhite Shelter Parking]. Turn right at the shelter, proceed behind the restroom building and parallel the creek. After about 0.25 mile the Trail will turn left, crossing the creek and emerging behind the Ox Roast Shelter. Continue north along the edge of the bluff, keeping the picnic area and open space to your left and the river to your right. After re-entering the woods from the edge of the picnic area, you will encounter the Watts Memorial Overlook [Watts Overlook] in Harrison Hills County Park.

The Watts Overlook is another good point at which to locate the Trail and has ample parking. Michael Watts was a Western Pennsylvania chemist who monitored the river for polluters and was active in environmental issues before they were as widely recognized as today. To find the Watts Overlook, enter Harrison Hills Park from

Freeport Road and bear left at the fork just beyond the park entrance. Follow the park road all the way to its end at the cul-de-sac [Ox Roast Shelter Parking]. There is ample parking just before you reach the cul-de-sac. The Overlook is approximately 150 yards to the left (north) of the cul-de-sac along the top of the bluff overlooking the Allegheny River.

From the Overlook, continue north along the edge of the bluff. Because this section runs along the edge of very steep bluffs you must watch your children and pets carefully. There are numerous points along this part of the Trail offering panoramic views that overlook the towns of the Allegheny Valley, especially when the leaves are off the trees. Stop often to enjoy the views.

After about a mile the Trail will intersect a gravel service road for a radio tower. Turn right and follow this road out to its intersection with Freeport Road. At this time, there is a sign at this location that says "Rachel Carson Trail" [Eastern Terminus]. This is the eastern terminus of the Trail.

Directly across Freeport Road, at its t-intersection of Millerstown Road [Parking ET], there is a parking area for at least three cars.

Trail Description East to West

**SECTION 7:
BURTNER
ROAD TO
EASTERN
TERMINUS**

6.8 mi. (10.9 km)

The eastern terminus of the Rachel Carson Trail is found just off Freeport Road in Harrison Township of Allegheny County. To reach it, take Route 28 to Exit 16. You will exit onto Millerstown Road; follow the signs in the direction of Freeport. Park your car at the t-intersection of Millerstown Road with Freeport Road [Parking ET]. There is a parking area here for at least three cars. If you are approaching this intersection on Freeport Road itself, Millerstown Road is not signed, but is located exactly 0.9 miles north of the entrance to Harrison Hills County Park on Freeport Road.

Note
Throughout this guide text in brackets, e.g. [Parking ET], indicates a reference to this location on the corresponding map for this trail section.

To locate the trailhead from the parking area, walk directly across Freeport Road and up a service road for a radio tower. At this time, there is a sign at this location that says "Rachel Carson Trail" [Eastern Terminus]. This is the eastern terminus of the Trail.

Follow the Trail, blazed with traffic yellow 2" by 6" rectangles away from Freeport Road and along the top of the hill. The Trail follows generally along the top edge of the bluff for 1.3 miles to the Watts Memorial Overlook [Watts Overlook] in Harrison Hills County Park. Because this first mile runs along the edge of very steep bluffs you must watch your children and pets carefully. There are numerous points along this part of the Trail offering panoramic views that overlook the towns of the Allegheny Valley, especially when the leaves are off the trees. Stop often to enjoy the views.

The Watts Overlook is another good point at which to locate the Trail and has ample parking. Michael Watts was a Western Pennsylvania chemist who monitored the river for polluters and was active in environmental issues before they were as widely recognized as today. To find the Watts Overlook, enter Harrison Hills Park from Freeport Road and bear left at the fork just beyond the park entrance. Follow the park road all the way to its end at the cul-de-sac [Ox Roast Shelter Parking]. There is ample parking just before you reach the cul-de-sac. The Overlook is approximately 150 yards to the left (north) of the cul-de-sac along the top of the bluff overlooking the Allegheny River.

From the Overlook, continue south along the edge of the bluff, keeping the picnic area and open space to your right and the river to your left; go behind the cul-de-sac and then go left, crossing a small creek as you turn back into the wooded area. On the other side of the creek, turn right, parallel the creek and emerge at the Bobwhite shelter, a terminus of the annual Rachel Carson Trail Challenge (described on page 1) and another place to locate the Trail [Bobwhite Shelter Parking]. The Trail skirts a small pond in which beavers have lived [Beaver Pond]. The Trail eventually comes out to Freeport Road about 50 yards the north of the Park entrance [HH Park Entrance]. Cross Freeport Road and follow the blazes turning to the right along a small side road running parallel to Freeport Road and leading to Altermoor Road, directly across Freeport Road from the Harrison Hills Volunteer Fire Department.

Turn left on Altermoor Road [Altermoor Road] and proceed for 1.5 blocks. Then turn left into the trees onto a gas line swath that doubles as an old dirt road. After about 100 yards, the Trail turns right and then goes to the bottom of the hill; then follow the yellow blazes to the left along the creek and through a marshy area and then upward toward a hilltop (elevation: 1300 ft.). Climb to the top of the hill and pass through the barbed wire, going in and then leaving a corral for the horses. Exiting the corral [Corral], find the Trail and head toward the houses down the hill. Follow the gravel driveway past several houses on your right to Alter Road [Alter Road]. Turn left onto Alter Road and walk to Saxonburg Road [Saxonburg Road]. Turn right (west) and walk along the left side of Saxonburg Road; go under the double overpass of Route 28.

Turn left (south) onto Donnelville Road [Donnelville Road], the first road to your left (no sign) and in less than 100 yards turn left again onto a cell tower service road leading uphill into the woods. In the fall the oaks and maples lining both sides of this lane and those that follow are especially beautiful. When the Trail reaches the top of the hill, you encounter the cell tower. Continue along left of the tower, then left again onto wide, open swath of a power line. Walk directly straight ahead across to the other side of the power line clearing. The Trail you want angles to the right into the woods, look for blazes before proceeding. Shortly the Trail comes back to the power line clearing; once again, cross directly in a straight line to the other side and find the blazes. For a third time, the Trail comes back to the power line clearing, and for the third time, cross over to the other side. The fourth time you encounter the power line clearing, do not cross over, rather, turn left and follow the tree line to the point where the Trail angles to the left into the woods. Spot the blazes! The Trail comes to another, older, power line, climbing southwest to a high point, elevation approximately 1240 feet, and eventually descends steeply and dramatically down to Burtner Road [Burtner Road].

SECTION 6: BAILEY RUN ROAD TO BURTNER ROAD
4.9 mi. (7.9 km)

Cross Burtner Road [Burtner Road] and climb the power line steeply to the top of the hill across the road. As you reach the top of the hill, the Trail goes to the left and proceeds through a wooded area. Turn right, as you reach the barbed wire fence, onto an old woods road. This section of the Trail is ablaze with fall colors in October. Reach Ridge Road [Ridge Road] at 0.9 miles from Burtner Road. Proceed south (left) on Ridge Road for 1.3 miles to Bull Creek Road [Bull Creek Road].

After crossing Bull Creek Road, turn left onto the berm of Bull Creek Road and walk towards Route 28 for approximately 220 yards. Before the overpass, turn right over the guardrail onto a path leading down through a hillside covered with crown vetch. The vetch is often quite thick, so take care not to get entangled. Bull Creek passes underneath you and the Expressway. Follow the path to an open area next to the Expressway, then head to the top of the ridge, looking for the Trail running along the hillside next to the treeline to your right, parallel to and within full view of the Expressway.

The top of the ridge [Tarentum Overlook] is a good spot to stop and enjoy the view of Route 28, exit number 14, and the town of Tarentum. When you are ready to leave, turn right relative to your route up the hillside, onto a jeep road and into the woods. The Trail then goes to the left and switchbacks down the hillside, crosses the creek, turns left and angles up the other side of the hill to Bakerstown Road [Bakerstown Road]. This wooded area is delightful in the summer and fall.

After reaching Bakerstown Road, turn right and walk along the road for 30 yards or so. Here the Trail cuts up into the hillside across the road at a reverse angle to your route; it zig-zags a couple of times back to a fence and follows the fence to the right to a point just above St. Clemens Cemetery [St. Clemens Cemetery]. The area from Bakerstown Road to the fence is often thickly overgrown with brambles. The Trail continues past a telecommunications tower, past another great view of the valley and then keeps to the left of a PPG tailings area. The Trail comes to a power line which merges in from your left and then very shortly verges into the woods to your right, descends a long hill down to the property of Roy Collins, past an abandoned house and to Bailey Run Road [Bailey Run Road]. Turn right (north) onto Bailey Run Road and shortly cross a small bridge. Continue left at the intersection immediately past the bridge. Continue along Bailey Run Road to the point where the Trail turns left off the road and over a guardrail.

SECTION 5: YUTES RUN ROAD TO BAILEY RUN ROAD
8.9 mi. (14.3 km)

Cross Bailey Run without using a bridge (usually a wet crossing). **Do not use any of the bridges of the local residents!** After crossing the stream, bear to your left, walking parallel to the stream for only 50 yards or so and then turn right going uphill into the trees and along the bed of a small stream descending through a crease in the hillside. You will pass a number of junk automobiles as you ascend the steep hill. The Trail continues up and around the hillside. As you approach a farm area (the farm of Jack Bailey), follow the blazes as the Trail takes a long detour around the farm clearing, keeping the farm to your right, going through a wooded area. As you come out into a power line clearing, enjoy the panoramic view to your right (north). The Trail goes back into the woods across the clearing and through an area that is covered with deep blue dayflowers with yellow whiskers in the summer. You soon come out onto the power line, continuing to the right and as you approach the Expressway, on your left, the Trail drops steeply down to Crawford Run Road [Crawford Run Road] in Creighton. Half way down this drop, watch for the Trail to lead back into the woods to your left for the last 100 yards before getting to the road. Turn left onto Crawford Run Road and follow the blazes along the road, under the overpass, past the highway ramp coming out on your right, to the rear of a small former schoolyard, also on your right.

This is a good spot to take a break if you are so inclined. There is a convenience store [Sheetz] adjacent to the schoolyard with food, drinks, and restrooms.

When you are ready to continue, go through the schoolyard, crossing Crawford Run on a small footbridge and then turning right onto Murray Hill Road [Murray Hill Road]. Walk about 200 yards up Murray Hill Road until you see the Trail turn left (east), off the road and steeply up the power line cut. (There may be a cable along the right tree line to assist you along here.) Follow the transmission lines downhill and then uphill, turning right into the woods as you approach Murray Hill Estates at the top of the hill. Cross two roads in that development, threading between backyards, to a field with a wooded area on the right. You will pass by a tall radio tower [Murray Hill Tower], immediately on your left; just beyond the tower the Trail enters some woods on your right. In only 150 yards or so the Trail comes out onto a jeep trail; turn right and follow this out to Murray Hill Road. Turn left for 0.2 miles until you reach Riddle Run Road [Riddle Run Road] and turn left again. Follow this road 0.8 miles to the entrance to Agan Park [Agan Park Entrance]. Turn left, pass the gate and head up the hill. This road leads up to the park ball fields. At the first intersection with another service road, turn left and follow it up the hill. The Trail soon turns right toward the bluffs and in less than 100 yards comes to the edge of the bluffs themselves. Go right along the top of the bluff. This section of the Trail offers terrific views of Arnold, New Kensington and Parnassus. In the distance one can see Lower Burrell and Plum Boro. Continue along the bluffs, observing the New Kensington bridge crossing the Allegheny River below. Although it is not evident that you are in a park, the park area offers a peaceful setting where you can take a break and (in the spring) enjoy the wildflowers. After turning left off the power line and into the woods and then back to the power line one more time, the Trail makes a dramatic drop down to the intersection of Freeport Road [Freeport Road] and Riddle Run Road (called Springdale Hollow Road on some maps) in Springdale.

Turn right (south) on Freeport Road [Freeport Road] and in less than 200 yards turn right again, leaving Freeport Road, traveling generally northwest and uphill along a gas pipeline which is soon joined by a power line. About halfway up the hill, you'll see the chain link fence surrounding playing fields for Springdale High School on your left [Springdale HS Fields].

Rachel Carson Homestead spur

To reach the Rachel Carson Homestead [Rachel Carson Homestead], walk along the perimeter of the chain link fence, heading away from the power line tower with a red band around it and following the red blazes on the posts. At the paved road, Butler Street, turn right and in about 200 yards left on Marion Avenue. Continue for 1.5 blocks and you will see the Homestead on the right side of the street, at 613 Marion Avenue. If you had turned left on Butler Street and walked downhill, you would have reached, in less than a block, the spring after which Springdale is named, still providing cold, clear spring water for thirsty hikers. The Homestead has been converted to an "ecology education center and museum". Springdale's pollution-monitoring station is located in the backyard.

Continue walking uphill along the pipeline/power line. The Trail goes up and down like a roller coaster several times. Soon after the pipeline bends to the left, the Trail leaves the pipeline, turning right into an attractive wooded area owned by William Shaul, who at one time was the milkman for the Carson family. When the Trail leaves the woods, you will see Butler Road [Butler Road] straight ahead. Cross Butler Road and onto the driveway leading up behind the greenhouse area of the former Peterson's Nursery. Continue up the hill on the paved driveway toward the house owned by Jim Drummond, taking the small left fork leading up to the orange globe marking the pipeline at the top of the hill. The Trail goes behind the ranch house to your right and within 250 yards the Trail turns left on a dirt road and heads toward a single house just inside the trees down the road. The Trail will turn to the right, away from the house just before reaching it, skirting the swimming pool of the house; keeping the pool to your left, go around behind the pool and then descend through a wooded area and, after crossing Tawney Run, out to Tawney Run Road [Tawney Run Road].

Cross Tawney Run Road into the trees on the other side of the road and turn left following an old railroad bed for a short distance. Then drop down to Tawney Run Road once again. Turn right on Tawney Run Road and continue along the road; turn right on Yutes Run Road [Yutes Run Road] in Harwick, the first road you encounter. Go under the Route 28 overpass and follow the road 0.7 miles.

**SECTION 4:
COVE RUN
ROAD TO
YUTES RUN
ROAD**
3.1 mi. (5 km)

Turn left off Yutes Run Road [Yutes Run Road] onto a gas pipeline steeply ascending the hill. Follow the gas pipeline up the steep hill and eventually you will descend to Log Cabin Road [Log Cabin Road]. Turn left on Log Cabin Road and walk 30 yards or so to Little Deer Creek Road, also called Russellton Road. Cross Little Deer Creek Road, continuing straight ahead on LaFever Hill Road [LaFever Hill Road] and go under a railroad bridge. At the second stone driveway on the right after the underpass, turn right; this drive leads to a refuse transfer station. In less than 30 yards turn left and go uphill following the gas pipeline once again. Follow the pipeline to the top of a ridge, keeping to the left edge of the woods along the pipeline swath. As you are approaching a house that appears to be a little to the left of the pipeline swath, up ahead, the Trail turns right into the woods - watch for the double blaze - and goes through a wooded area (basically going around the private property associated with the house up ahead). As you exit the wooded area you encounter a paved road running from uphill on your left and going downhill to a fly ash dump site on your right. Turn left, walking uphill along the road; at the top of the hill follow along the right side of the chain link fence, then turn right and head down the dirt road. When you encounter the pipeline swath once again, turn left and follow it to Rich Hill Road [Rich Hill Road], another quarter mile or so further down the Trail.

Cross Rich Hill Road, continue straight ahead and make the treacherous descent down to Long Run [Long Run], continuing to follow the pipeline. Just after crossing Long Run, turn left into a beautiful section which is full of wildflowers in spring (notably fire pinks and trillium). Unfortunately this area has been attacked by trail bikes, but you can enjoy the wildflowers alongside the Trail anyway. Follow the Trail upward through the woods, ascending to the top of a hill and then descending down the other side of the hill to a paved road, Cove Run Road [Cove Run Road].

**SECTION 3:
SHAFFER
ROAD TO
COVE RUN
ROAD**
4.6 mi. (7.4 km)

Cross Cove Run Road [Cove Run Road] and continue through an area that again shares the Trail with trail bikes. Some of the trail bike ruts in this area are quite deep. As you leave a cleared area about 100 yards past Cove Run Road and enter the woods the Trail bears to the left into Emmerling Park and descends through a magnificent stand of hemlocks to Deer Creek. Cross Deer Creek using the bridge [Deer Creek Bridge] installed by Indiana Township, turn right and follow the woodchip path along the creek. Emmerling Park is an Indiana Township Park with rest rooms, picnic shelters, and ball fields.

After reaching the parking lot, turn right and cross the footbridge out to Cove Run Road. Cross over onto Eisele Road [Eisele Road]. Walk along Eisele Road past Camp Deer Creek on your left, then past the pipeline swath to a jeep trail on the left, 0.7 miles from the intersection with Cove Run Road. In May, look for spectacular European columbine along Eisele Road and on the wooded section that follows. The path descends into a wooded area a little ways past the last house near the top of the hill. At the bottom of the hill turn left before crossing the stream and continue downstream passing the familiar pipeline swath that ascends steeply up the hill on your left. Here, cross the small stream called Cunningham Run (usually a wet crossing) and continue about 50 yards to the crane equipment tool yard [Casey Equipment]. Walk through the warehouse grounds (stay off the equipment) and go to the right along its entrance driveway to get to Saxonburg Boulevard near Dorseyville [Saxonburg Boulevard]. After passing through the gate at the driveway entrance, turn left and head diagonally across the grassy field toward the road.

Turn left on Saxonburg Boulevard and cross Deer Creek on a bridge. Continue on this road for about 0.5 miles, crossing over the Pennsylvania Turnpike. As you approach the intersection with Route 910, the Trail makes a right turn over the guardrail down and into the woods and crosses property owned by Tom Eichenlaub. It emerges on Route 910 [Route 910], turns right and follows 910 to the first intersection which is Cedar Run Road [Cedar Run Road]. Turn left (west) onto Cedar Run Road and continue along Cedar Run Road to the junction in 0.4 miles with Shaffer Road [Shaffer Road]. Bear left (west) onto Shaffer Road, a lightly traveled road that soon turns to gravel and ends when it intersects Church Lane.

SECTION 2: ROUTE 8 TO SHAFFER ROAD
3.2 mi (5.1 km)

Turn right on Church Lane [Church Lane] and in about 350 yards turn left onto the unpaved Wagner Road [Wagner Road]. The Trail will turn right, leaving the road, in only 200 yards, now 1.4 miles from Route 910, at the left edge of a parking area and to the right of a small pond. (Do not park your car here, it's private property.) Follow along the right side of the creek until you can cross over a dirt bridge (atop a large pipe). On the other side of the creek, turn right and head up a small hillside. Please stay on the Trail in this area and do not approach the houses (the landowners here appreciate their privacy). When you come out of the trees into an open field area, head toward a clump of pine trees straight ahead that you will discover surround a small private lake [Hidden Pond]. This is an excellent spot to enjoy lunch in the small pavilion built by the owner, Nicola DiCio. When leaving the lake, you encounter an area cleared of trees where the Trail is difficult to locate. Head up the small hill from the pavilion almost immediately turn left. Proceed just below the tree line on your right until, after 150 yards or so, you locate the Trail going up into the trees to your right.

Hartwood Acres spur

At this point, where the Trail leaves the field and enters the woods, Hartwood Acres can be reached by a trail going off from this point to the other side (south) of Wagner Road. Look for a 4"x4" post with a red band around it. Head down the hill and across the field to the next red blaze on a pole. At Wagner road turn left and then right down Edgehill Drive. At the back end of Edgehill Drive (see a sign "TRAIL" with an arrow), follow up a dirt path to the right which leads off behind the paved driveway, then on the limestone chip road to the left of the corral fence and up to the Hartwood Acres mansion. The spur exits into an open grassy area behind a dome shaped maintenance building, several hundred feet from the mansion.

Proceed up through a wooded area to a 1300 ft. knob on a cleared hilltop. Continuing into a private yard, stay right and follow the tree line on the right while coming down the hill, and go in the shortest line to the road ahead, Cedar Run Road. Turn left on this road, cross Middle Road [Middle Road] onto McCully Road [McCully Road] and continue straight ahead on McCully Road until just before it begins to descend. Watch carefully for a quick right turn (north) up an incline and into the Hampton Nature Reserve. Follow the Trail in this Reserve for more than 1.0 mile first to a small stream at the bottom of the hill, over a footbridge and then uphill where you encounter and cross another utility right-of-way. Going through some woods and along a dirt lane, you reach a Hampton Township school property where you come out of the trees into an open field. Follow along the right edge of the field onto an old road near a small section of guardrail. The Trail follows this road a short distance then turns left into the woods. The Trail comes out to a paved road [Topnick Drive] where you cross the road, go right, and then go left over the guardrail into more woods in less than 100 yards. The Trail will take you uphill to the corner of Hampton Middle School property [School Road]. When you first leave the woods, you see another nice place for a break or lunch, under the shade trees on the school lawn. Turn left on the paved street at the top of the hill just out of the woods and walk along the left side of the roadway parallel to the school building on your right and walk around to the rear of the building. At the rear of the building the Trail leaves the school property via a path to your left, going downhill into some bushes and alongside a private house, onto its driveway out to PA Route 8, just south of a car dealership [Route 8]. This area is known as Talley Cavey.

**SECTION 1:
WESTERN
TERMINUS TO
ROUTE 8**
4.3 mi. (6.9 km)

Cross PA Route 8 [Route 8]. The safest way to do this is to go to the stop light at the intersection to your right, about 200 yards down the road. This is a heavily traveled road with fast-moving traffic. The Trail enters the woods directly opposite the pathway to PA Route 8. Once you are across Route 8, traverse private property first passing a detention pond to your left in the dense bushes and then passing closely behind several houses. Just after crossing a small gravel roadway [Indian Springs Lane], the Trail passes around a gate ("No Trespassing" signs may be posted), follows the treeline for about 50 feet and then descends into the Crouse Run area (you will observe the grade of the former Pittsburgh-to-Butler Interurban running parallel to Crouse Run). The Trail crosses Crouse Run several times (wet crossings), going onto and off the railroad grade. The Trail goes up to Sample Road [Sample Road] at a small gravel parking area [Sample Road Parking] in an area called Sample Station. Turn right on Sample Road and cross Pine Creek on a bridge; continue 250 yards along Sample Road to a railroad track crossing. Turn right after crossing the tracks and follow the Trail keeping to the left (south) side of the tracks. In about a quarter mile, turn left into the trees and follow the stream all the way to the abandoned Rocky Dell Shelter [Rocky Dell Shelter] in North Park. The rocky ledges in the shelter area are worth a few photographs. From the shelter, go up the hillside on crude steps to Hemlocks Drive III. At the road, turn left, go 50 yards or so down the road and turn right on the dirt road leading up the hill.

Take the dirt road to the top of the hill. Just before you reach the paved road the Trail cuts to the left, through a short stretch of woods and then crosses the paved road over into the Beveridge Picnic Shelter area. Go to the left of the Beveridge Shelter and in about 100 yards pass to the right of the Elwood Shelter. The Trail will cross another paved road at a point 50 yards to the right of the Woods Athletic Field and cut a course across that road that is about halfway between the Jeanette Shelter on your right and the Lilac Shelter on your left. Just after passing these two shelters you will see the Triple Oak Shelter to your right. Soon you see the Honeysuckle Shelter on your right with the road to your left. You then pass to the rear and to the right of the Harmar Shelter. The Trail continues through the woods and in quick succession passes to the left of the Tupelo Shelter and then to the right and behind the Massachusetts Shelter.

The Trail then descends the hillside down past the Connolly Shelter on your far left, and connects with the park road leading out to a junction with Wildwood Road [Wildwood Road]. Cross Wildwood Road and continue straight ahead on a driveway leading back to The Mansions condominium development. In only 100 yards or so when the pavement turns right, continue somewhat to the left onto the dirt path leading over to Pine Creek which flows out of North Park Lake. The path keeps Pine Creek to your left and soon reaches Babcock Boulevard [Babcock Boulevard]. Turn right and follow Babcock Boulevard briefly to its intersection with Pearce Mill Road (also Pierce Mill Road) where you turn left and walk along the right side of Pierce Mill Road for only 100 yards. Just past the small lake on your right, turn right up toward the picnic area and walk along with the lake to your right. This area in here is usually low and soggy. Just as you pass the small lake you will see a causeway coming in from the right with the lake on one side and a marshy area on the other intersecting your trail. The "Rachel Carson Trail" [Western Terminus] signpost you see at this location is the western terminus of the Trail. If you turn right and cross over the causeway to the Beaver Shelter you will come to a North Park parking area along Babcock Boulevard [Parking WT]. This shelter is also a terminus of the annual Rachel Carson Trail Challenge. You may alternatively continue straight ahead and follow the well-defined bridle trail all the way to the North Park Skating Rink, another 2.2 miles further. It has been reported (9/97) that maps of North Park incorrectly show the bridle trail leading to the Skating Rink as the Rachel Carson Trail.

Section 1: Western Terminus to Route 8

Trail Distance 4.3 miles (6.9 km)

Section 2: Route 8 to Shaffer Road

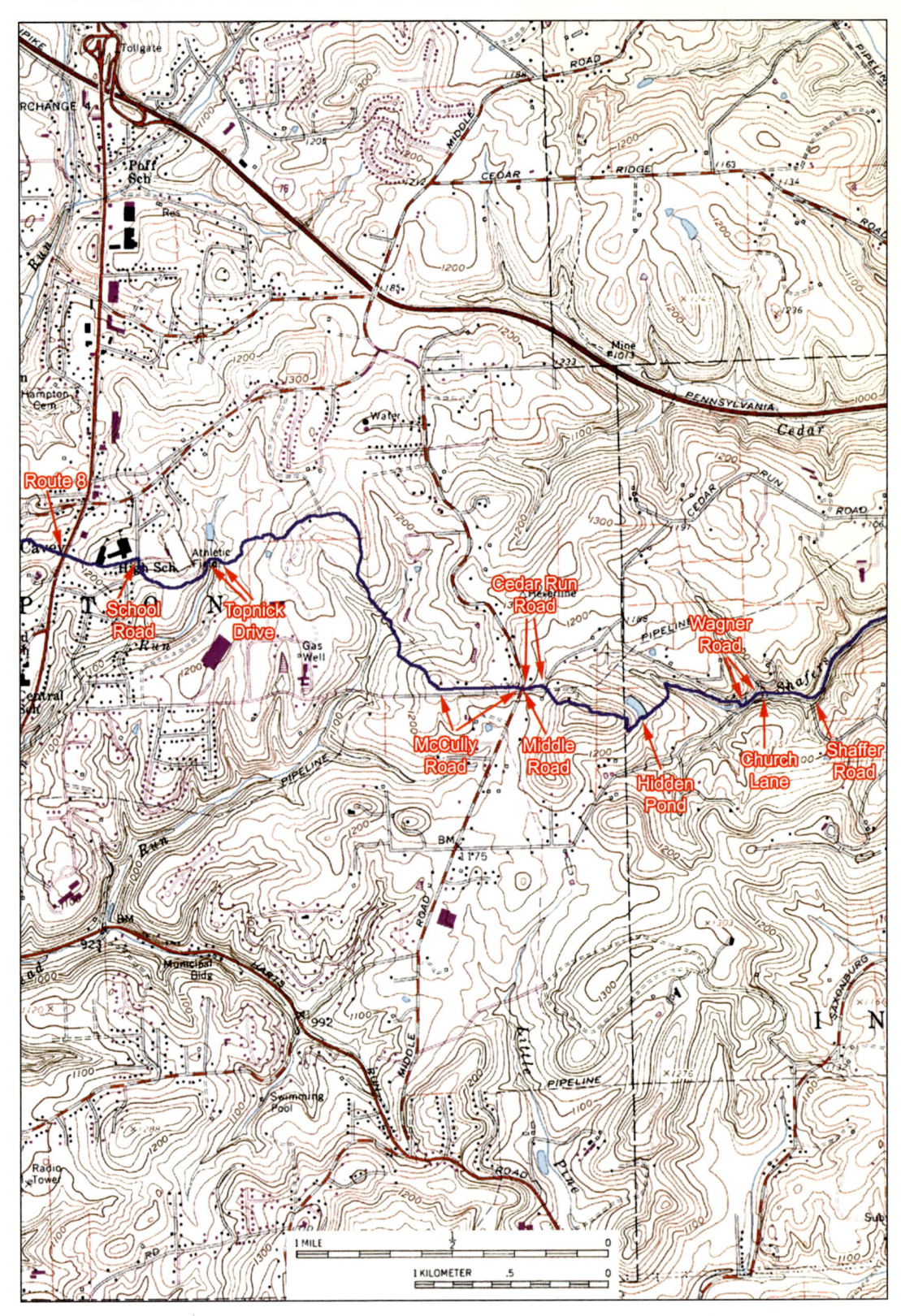

Trail Distance 3.2 miles (5.1 km)

Section 3: Shaffer Road to Cove Run Road

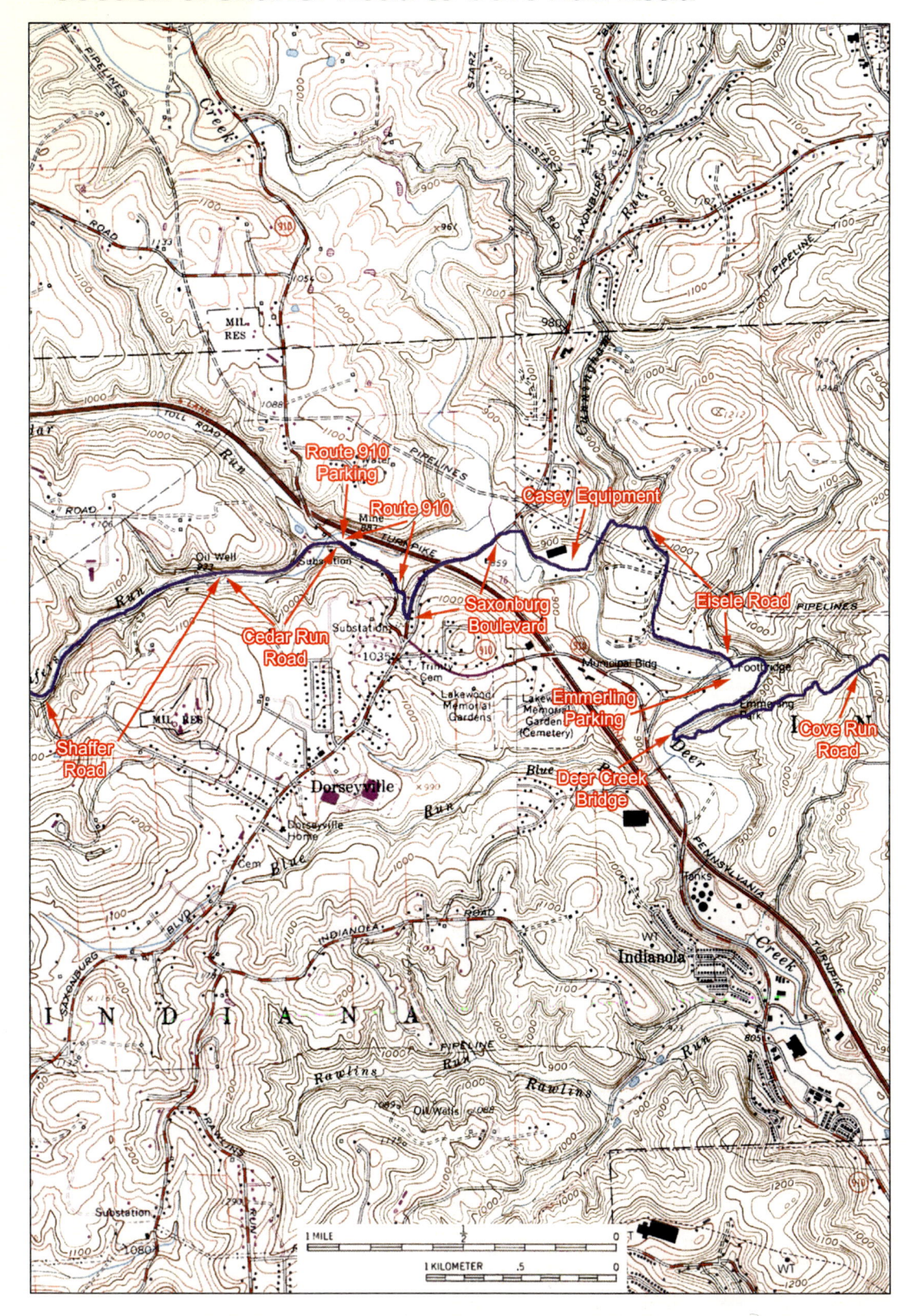

Trail Distance 4.6 miles (7.4 km)

Section 4: Cove Run Road to Yutes Run Road

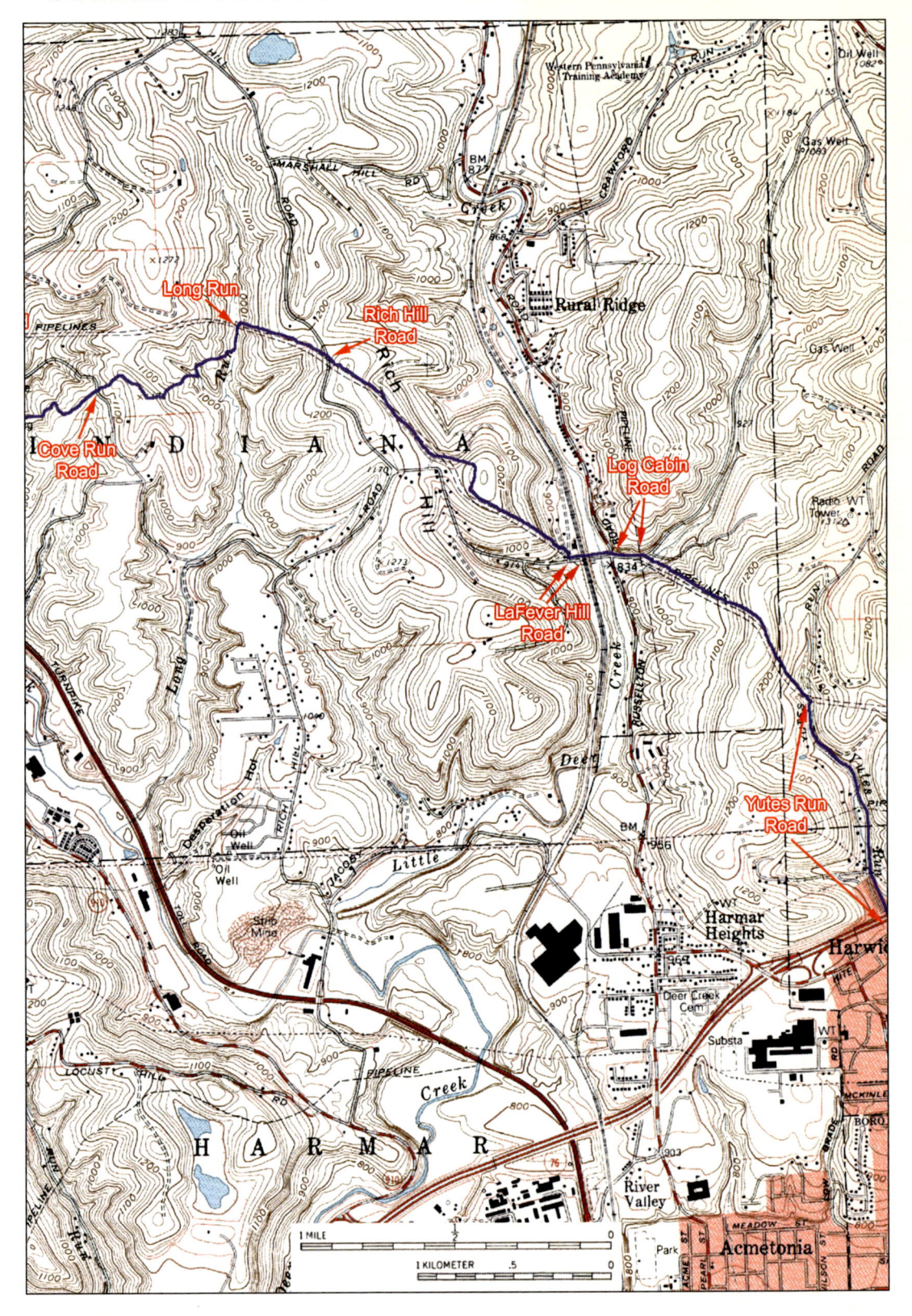

Trail Distance 3.1 miles (5 km)

Section 5: Yutes Run Road to Bailey Run Road

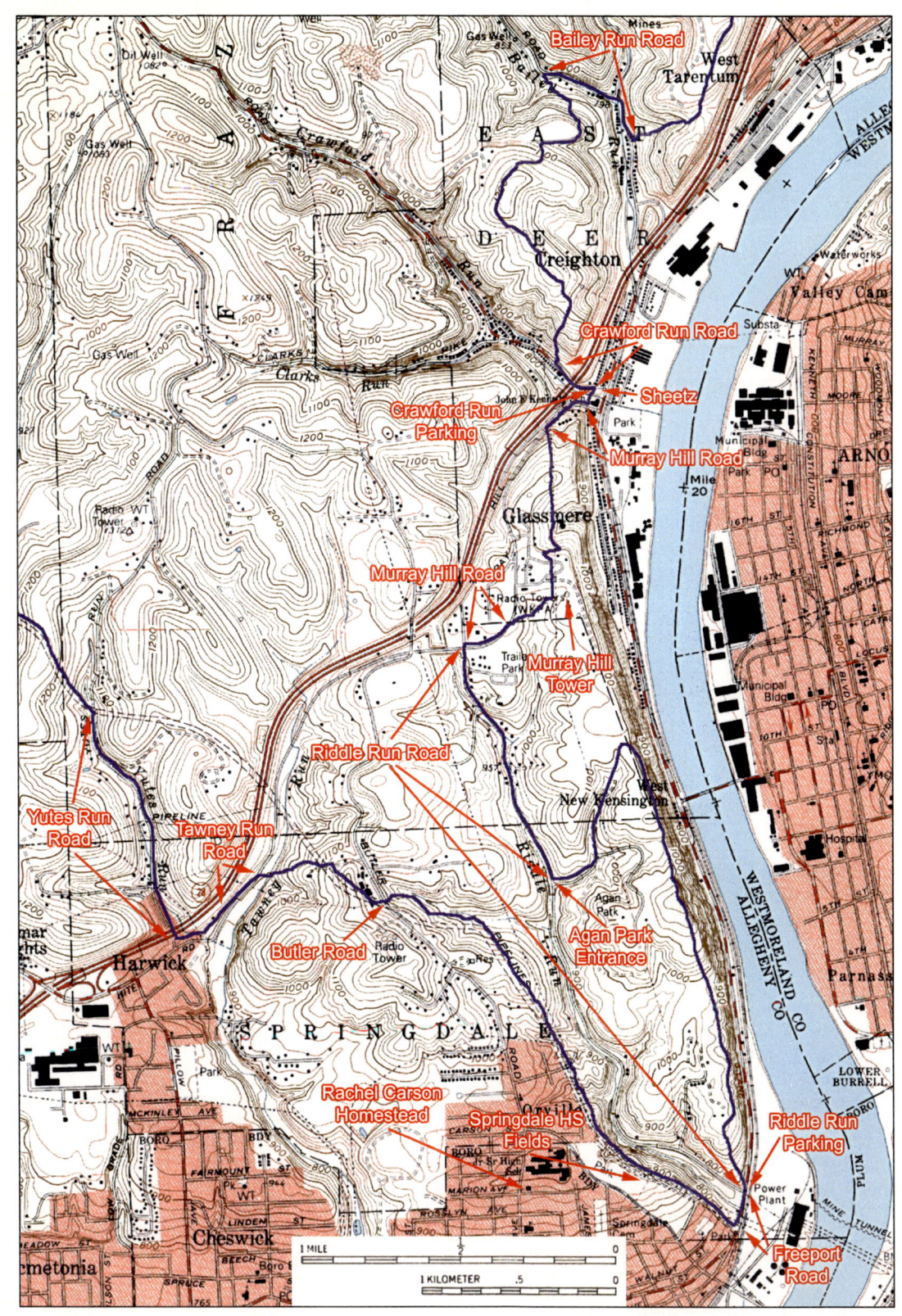

Trail Distance 8.9 miles (14.3 km)

Section 6: Bailey Run Road to Burtner Road

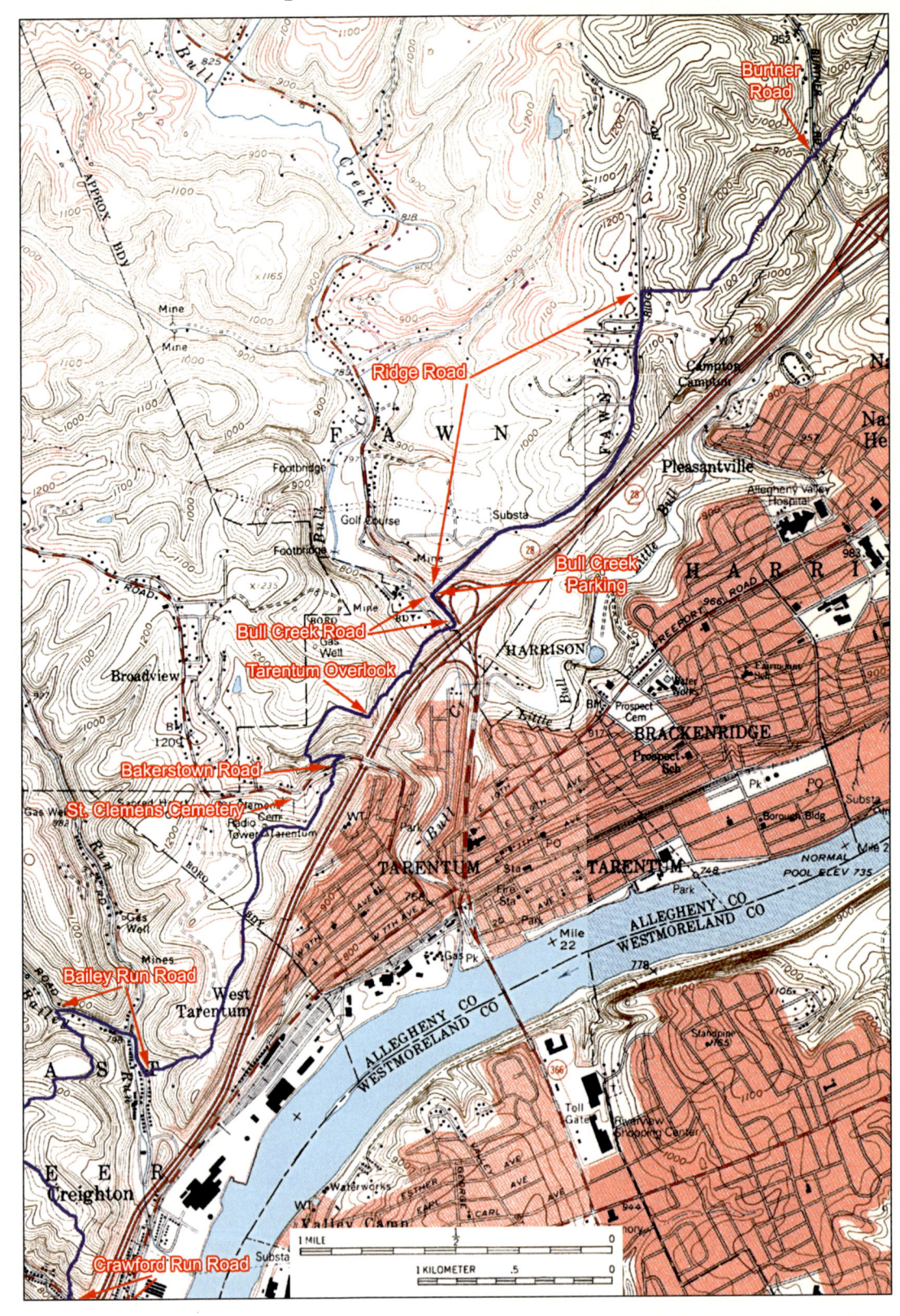

Trail Distance 4.9 miles (7.9 km)

Section 7: Burtner Road to Eastern Terminus

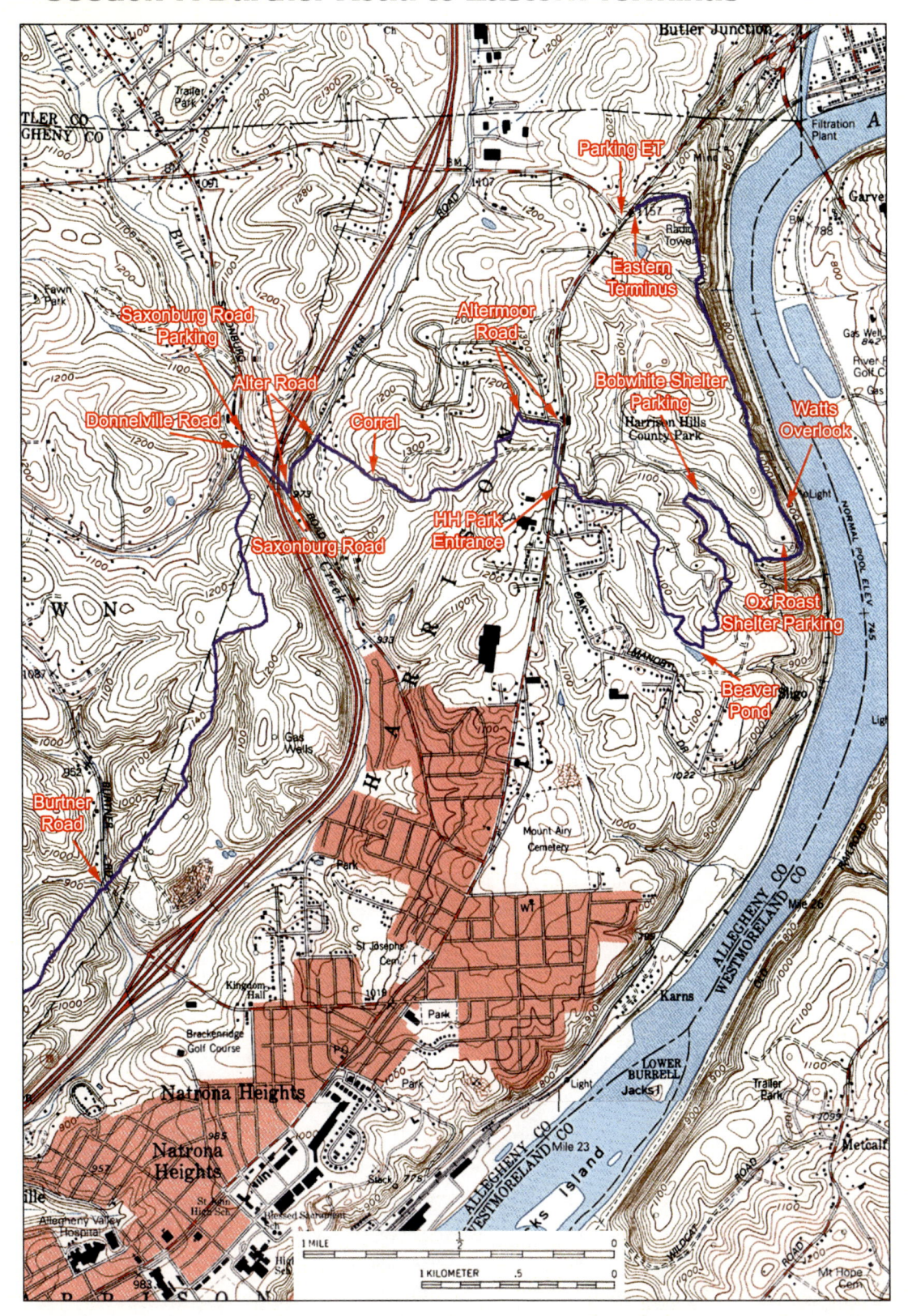

Trail Distance 6.8 miles (10.9 km)

Table of GPS Coordinates

This table provides the GPS (Global Positioning System) coordinates for various points along the Trail. The coordinate datum is WGS84.

Key	Location	Coordinates
Parking ET	Parking area across from eastern trailhead at intersection of Millerstown Rd. and Freeport Rd. with space for 3+ cars.	40° 39.921' N 79° 42.222' W
Watts Overlook	Bluff along Trail above Allegheny River at Michael Watts Memorial.	40° 39.114' N 79° 41.636' W
Ox Roast Shelter Parking	Parking area at the Ox Roast Shelter in Harrison Hills Park with space for 15+ cars.	40° 39.028' N 79° 41.663' W
Bobwhite Shelter Parking	Parking area along Trail at the Bobwhite Shelter in Harrison Hills Park with space for 100+ cars.	40° 39.189' N 79° 41.963' W
Saxonburg Road Parking	Parking area along Trail at intersection of Donnelville Rd. and Saxonburg Rd. with space for 2+ cars.	40° 39.303' N 79° 43.613' W
Bull Creek Parking	Parking area along Trail at intersection of Ridge Rd. and Bull Creek Rd. with space for 15+ cars.	40° 36.915' N 79° 45.529' W
Tarentum Overlook	Ridge above Route 28 and Tarentum.	40° 36.578' N 79° 45.782' W
Crawford Run Parking	Parking area along Trail on Crawford Run Rd. behind Sheetz with space for 8+ cars.	40° 34.937' N 79° 46.756' W
Agan Park Entrance	Parking area along Trail at entrance to Agan Park with space for 6+ cars.	40° 33.600' N 79° 46.916' W
Riddle Run Parking	Parking area along Trail at intersection of Riddle Run Rd. and Freeport Rd. with space for 8+ cars.	40° 32.765' N 79° 46.243' W
Emmerling Parking	Parking area along Trail off Cove Run Rd. in Emmerling Park with space for 50+ cars.	40° 34.931' N 79° 51.668' W
Route 910 Parking	Parking area along Trail off Route 910 at River City Glass with space for 5 cars. Please park next to 910 between the buildings.	40° 35.271' N 79° 53.080' W
Sample Road Parking	Parking area along trail on Sample Rd. at Crouse Run with space for 2 cars.	40° 34.796' N 79° 58.022' W
Parking WT	Parking area near western trailhead off Babcock Blvd. in North Park with space for 100+ cars.	40° 35.968' N 79° 59.788' W

Directions to the Trailheads

WESTERN TRAILHEAD

From Pittsburgh, take I279 North to the McKnight Road exit and travel 6.4 miles north. Take the North Park/Ingomar Rd. exit east and turn left at the third traffic light onto Babcock Blvd. The parking lot is on the left at the next intersection with Pearce Mill Road (aka Pierce Mill Road), and the Beaver Shelter is at the far end of the lot. The trailhead is in the woods across the causeway.

From northwest/southwest, take I79 to Mt. Nebo Road exit 68. Turn east (left if exiting southbound) on Mt. Nebo road, and then left onto Arndt Road at the traffic light. At the T intersection with Reis Run Road turn left. After about 4.3 miles you will pass beneath the McKnight Road overpass. Continue straight and turn left at the third traffic light onto Babcock Blvd. The parking lot is on the left at the next intersection with Pearce Mill Road (aka Pierce Mill Road), and the Beaver Shelter is at the far end of the lot. The trailhead is in the woods across the causeway.

From the turnpike, exit at interchange 39. After the tollbooth, bear right toward Butler and immediately upon entering Route 8 merge into the left lane and turn left at first traffic light onto West Hardies Road. Follow it two miles to the first traffic light and turn right onto Wildwood Road. At the next traffic light turn right again. The parking lot is on the left at the next intersection with Pearce Mill Road (aka Pierce Mill Road), and the Beaver Shelter is at the far end of the lot. The trailhead is in the woods across the causeway.

EASTERN TRAILHEAD

From Pittsburgh/northeast, take Route 28 to exit 16, turn east (right if exiting northbound) at the end of the ramp onto Millerstown Road and follow it to the T intersection with Freeport Road. There is a parking area on the left at this intersection for at least 3 cars. The trailhead is directly across Freeport Road.

From the turnpike, exit at interchange 48. After the tollbooth, bear right onto Freeport Road toward Pittsburgh. After 0.5 miles turn right onto Route 910 at the traffic light. After about 1,000 feet bear right onto Route 28 north. Follow it to exit 16, turn right at the end of the ramp onto Millerstown Road and follow it to the T intersection with Freeport Road. There is a parking area on the left at this intersection for at least 3 cars. The trailhead is directly across Freeport Road.

Index

Agan Park Entrance, 13, 19, **29**
Alter Road, 15, 18, **31**
Altermoor Road, 15, 18, **31**
American Youth Hostels, 1
Babcock Boulevard, 9, 24
Bailey Run Road, 14, 19, **29**, **30**
Baker Trail, 1
Bakerstown Road, 18, **30**
Beaver Pond, 15, 17, **31**
blazes, 3
    Double blaze, 3
    Single blaze, 3
Bobcock Boulevard, **25**
Bobwhite Shelter Parking, 15, 17, **31**
Bruce Schenker, 4
Bull Creek Parking, **30**
Bull Creek Road, 14, 18, **30**
Burtner Road, 18, **30**, **31**
Butler Road, 12, 20, **29**
Casey Equipment, 11, 22, **27**
Cedar Run Road, 11, 22, **26**, **27**
Church Lane, 11, 22, **26**
Cliff Ham, 4
Corral, 15, 18, **31**
Cove Run Road, 21, **27**, **28**
Crawford Run Parking, **29**
Crawford Run Road, 13, 19, **29**
Crouse Run, 10, 23
Deer Creek Bridge, 11, 21, **27**
Donnelville Road, 15, 18, **31**
Eastern Terminus, 16, 17
Eisele Road, 11, 21, **27**
Emmerling Park, 11, 21
Emmerling Parking, **27**
Freeport Road, 17, 20, **29**
Hampton Middle School, 10, 23
Hampton Nature Reserve, 1, 23
Harmony Trails Council, 7
Harrison Hills County Park, 1, 17
Hartwood Acres, 10, 22
Hartwood Acres County Park, 1
Hemlocks Drive III, 9, 23
HH Park Entrance, 15, 17, **31**
Hidden Pond, 11, 22, **26**
Indian Springs Lane, 10, 23, **25**
Jim Drummond, 12, 20
LaFever Hill Road, 12, 21, **28**
Little Deer Creek Road, 12, 21
Log Cabin Road, 12, 21, **28**
Long Run, 12, 21, **28**
Marilyn Ham, 4
McCully Road, 10, 23, **26**
Michael Watts, 15, 17
Middle Road, 10, 23, **26**

Millerstown Road, 16, 17, 33
Murray Hill Road, 13, 19, **29**
Murray Hill Tower, 13, 19, **29**
Nicola DiCio, 11, 22
North Country Trail, 1
North Park, 1
Ox Roast Shelter Parking, 16, 17, **31**
Parking ET, 16, 17, **31**
Parking WT, 9, 24, **25**
Pearce Mill Road, 9, 24, 33
Pierce Mill Road. *See* Pearce Mill Road
Pine Creek, 9, 23, 24
Pittsburgh-to-Butler Interurban, 10, 23
PPG tailings area, 14, 19
Rachel Carson Homestead, 6, 12, 20, **29**
Rachel Carson Trail Challenge, 1, 9, 24
Rachel Carson Trails Conservancy, 7
Rachel Louise Carson, 5
Rich Hill Road, 12, 21, **28**
Riddle Run Parking, **29**
Riddle Run Road, 19, **29**
Ridge Road, 14, 18, **30**
Rocky Dell Shelter, 1, 9, 23, **25**
Route 8, 23, **25**, **26**
Route 910, 11, 22, **27**
Route 910 Parking, **27**
Russellton Road, 21
Sample Road, 10, 23, **25**
Sample Road Parking, **25**
Sample Station, 9, 23
Saxonburg Boulevard, 22, **27**
Saxonburg Road, 15, 18, **31**
Saxonburg Road Parking, **31**
School Road, 10, 23, **26**
Shaffer Road, 11, 22, **26**, **27**
Sheetz, 13, 19, **29**
Silent Spring, 5
Springdale HS Fields, 12, 20, **29**
St. Clemens Cemetery, 14, 19, **30**
Talley Cavey, 10, 23
Tarentum Overlook, 14, 18, **30**
Tawney Run Road, 12, 21, **29**
terminus
    eastern, 17, **31**, 33
    western, 9, 24, **25**, 33
The Mansions, 24
The Sea Around Us, 5
Tom Eichenlaub, 11, 22
Topnick Drive, 10, 23, **26**
Wagner Road, 11, 22, **26**
Watts Overlook, 15, 17, **31**
Western Terminus, 9, 24
Wildwood Road, 24, **25**
Yutes Run Road, 12, 21, **28**, **29**

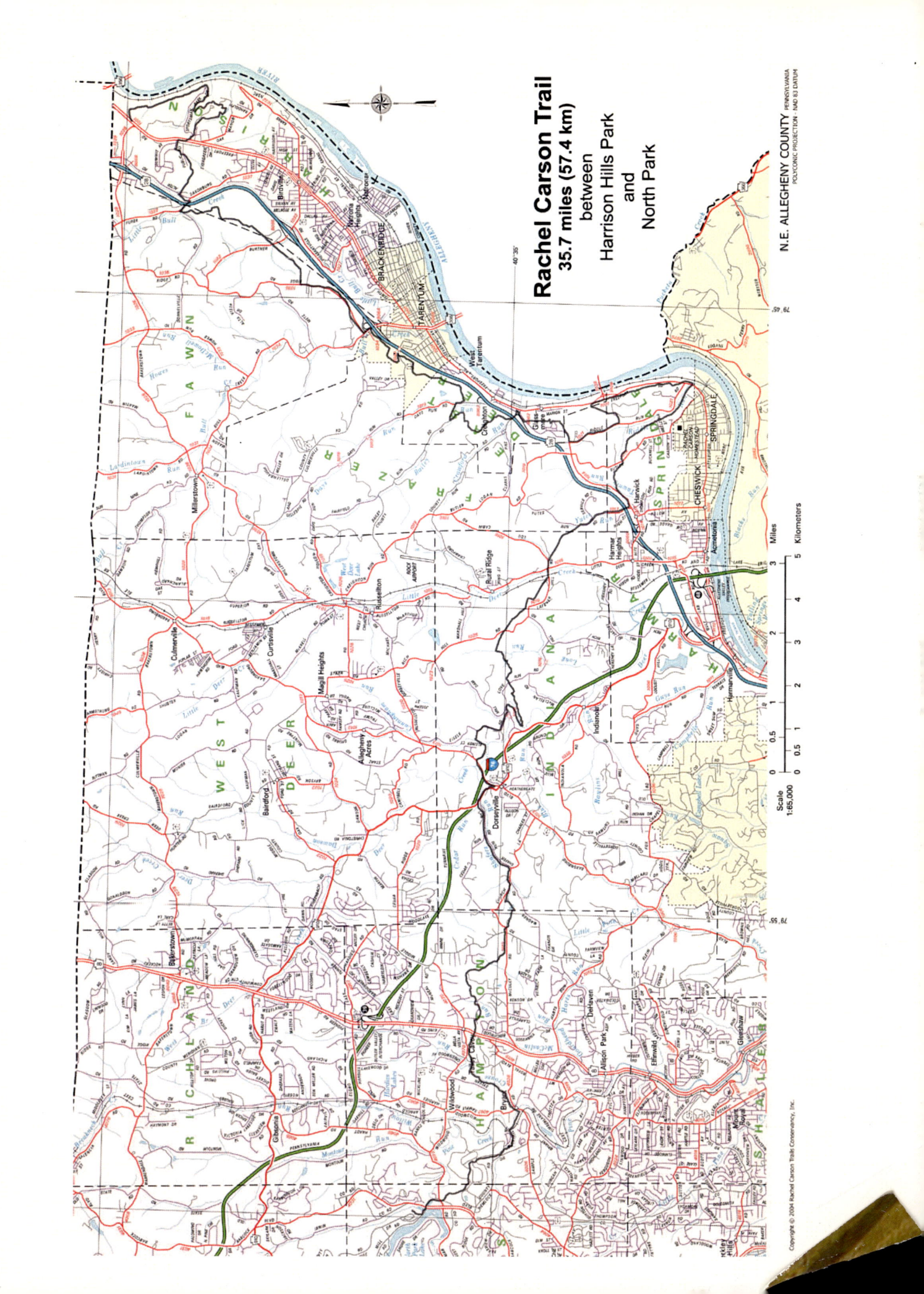

Rachel Carson Trail
35.7 miles (57.4 km)
between
Harrison Hills Park
and
North Park

A secret world awaits you.
A world on the periphery of your world.
A world of quiet woods, cool valleys, ageless streams, and undulating hills.
A world that can change your perspective on things you see every day.
On what you take for granted every day.
The Rachel Carson Trail awaits you.

ISBN 1-59571-065-5

$14.95

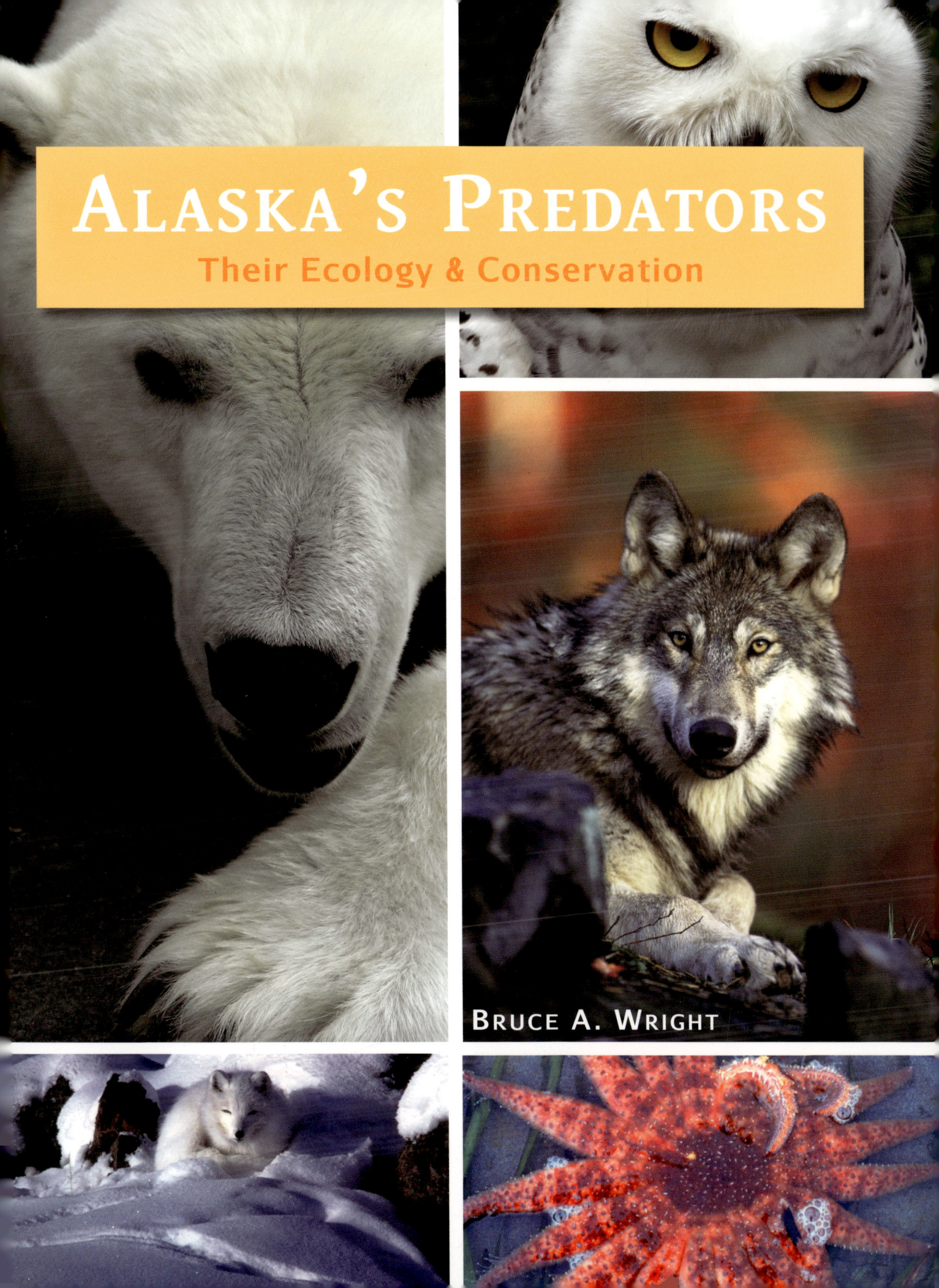

Alaska's Predators
Their Ecology & Conservation

Bruce A. Wright